vi Editor
Pocket Reference

vi Editor
Pocket Reference

Arnold Robbins

Beijing • Cambridge • Farnham • Köln • Paris • Sebastopol • Taipei • Tokyo

vi Editor Pocket Reference

by Arnold Robbins

Copyright © 1999 O'Reilly & Associates, Inc. All rights reserved.
Printed in the United States of America. Published by O'Reilly &
Associates, Inc., 1005 Gravenstein Highway North, Sebastopol,
CA 95472.

Editor: Gigi Estabrook

Production Editor: Mary Anne Weeks Mayo

Cover Design: Edie Freedman

Printing History:

January 1999:   First Edition

ISBN: 1-56592-497-5
[C]   [3/03]

Table of Contents

vi Editor Pocket Reference

Introduction

This pocket reference is a companion to *Learning the vi Editor*, by Linda Lamb and Arnold Robbins. It describes the *vi* command-line options, command mode commands, *ex* commands and options, regular expressions and the use of the substitute (s) command, and other pertinent information for using *vi*. Also covered are the additional features in the four *vi* clones, *nvi*, *elvis*, *vim*, and *vile*.

The Solaris 2.6 version of *vi* served as the "reference" version of *vi* for this pocket reference.

Conventions

The following font conventions are used in this book:

Courier

> Used for command names, options, and everything to be typed literally

Courier Italic

> Used for replaceable text within commands

Italic

> Used for replaceable text within regular text, program names, filenames, paths, for emphasis, and new terms when first defined

[...]

> Identifies optional text; the brackets are not typed

CTRL-G

> Indicates a keystroke

1. Command-Line Options

Command	Action
vi *file*	Invoke *vi* on *file*
vi *file1 file2*	Invoke *vi* on files sequentially
view *file*	Invoke *vi* on *file* in read-only mode
vi -R *file*	Invoke *vi* on *file* in read-only mode
vi -r *file*	Recover *file* and recent edits after a crash
vi -t *tag*	Look up *tag* and start editing at its definition
vi -w *n*	Set the window size to *n*; useful over a slow connection
vi + *file*	Open *file* at last line
vi +n *file*	Open *file* directly at line number *n*
vi -c *command file*	Open *file*, execute *command*, which is usually a search command or line number (POSIX)
vi +/*pattern file*	Open *file* directly at *pattern*
ex *file*	Invoke *ex* on *file*
ex - *file* < *script*	Invoke *ex* on *file*, taking commands from *script*; suppress informative messages and prompts
ex -s *file* < *script*	Invoke *ex* on *file*, taking commands from *script*; suppress informative messages and prompts (POSIX)

2. vi Commands

Most *vi* commands follow a general pattern:

[*command*][*number*]text object

or the equivalent form:

[*number*][*command*]text object

Movement Commands

Command	Meaning
Character	
h, j,	
k, l	Left, down, up, right ($\leftarrow$, $\downarrow$, $\uparrow$, $\rightarrow$)
Text	
w, W,	
b, B	Forward, backward by word
e, E	End of word
), (	Beginning of next, previous sentence
}, {	Beginning of next, previous paragraph
]], [[	Beginning of next, previous section
Lines	
RETURN	First nonblank character of next line
0, $	First, last position of current line
^	First nonblank character of current line
+, -	First nonblank character of next, previous line
n |	Column *n* of current line
H	Top line of screen
M	Middle line of screen
L	Last line of screen

Command	Meaning
nH	*n* (number) of lines after top line
nL	*n* (number) of lines before last line

Scrolling

Command	Meaning
CTRL-F , CTRL-B	Scroll forward, backward one screen
CTRL-D , CTRL-U	Scroll down, up one-half screen
CTRL-E , CTRL-Y	Show one more line at bottom, top of window
z RETURN	Reposition line with cursor: to top of screen
z .	Reposition line with cursor: to middle of screen
z -	Reposition line with cursor: to bottom of screen
CTRL-L	Redraw screen (without scrolling)

Searches

Command	Meaning
/pattern	Search forward for *pattern*
?pattern	Search backward for *pattern*
n, N	Repeat last search in same, opposite direction
/, ?	Repeat previous search forward, backward
fx	Search forward for character *x* in current line
Fx	Search backward for character *x* in current line
tx	Search forward to character before *x* in current line
Tx	Search backward to character after *x* in current line
;	Repeat previous current-line search
,	Repeat previous current-line search in opposite direction

Command	Meaning
Line number	
CTRL-G	Display current line number
nG	Move to line number *n*
G	Move to last line in file
:n	Move to line *n* in file
Marking position	
mx	Mark current position as *x*
`x	Move cursor to mark *x*
` `	Return to previous mark or context
'x	Move to beginning of line containing mark *x*
' '	Return to beginning of line containing previous mark

Editing Commands

Command	Action
Insert	
i, a	Insert text before, after cursor
I, A	Insert text before beginning, after end of line
o, O	Open new line for text below, above cursor
Change	
r	Replace character
cw	Change word
cc	Change current line
cmotion	Change text between the cursor and the target of *motion*
C	Change to end of line
R	Type over (overwrite) characters

Command	Action
s	Substitute: delete character and insert new text
S	Substitute: delete current line and insert new text
Delete, move	
x	Delete character under cursor
X	Delete character before cursor
dw	Delete word
dd	Delete current line
d*motion*	Delete text between the cursor and the target of *motion*
D	Delete to end of line
p, P	Put deleted text after, before cursor
"*n*p	Put text from delete buffer number *n* after cursor (for last nine deletions)
Yank	
yw	Yank (copy) word
yy	Yank current line
"*a*yy	Yank current line into named buffer *a* (a–z). Uppercase names append text
y*motion*	Yank text between the cursor and the target of *motion*
p, P	Put yanked text after, before cursor
"*a*P	Put text from buffer *a* before cursor (a–z)
Other commands	
.	Repeat last edit command
u, U	Undo last edit; restore current line
J	Join two lines
ex edit commands	
:d	Delete lines

Command	Action
:m	Move lines
:co or :t	Copy lines
:.,$d	Delete from current line to end of file
:30,60m0	Move lines 30 through 60 to top of file
:.,/pattern/co$	Copy from current line through line containing *pattern* to end of file

Exit Commands

Command	Meaning
ZZ	Write (save) and quit file
:x	Write (save) and quit file
:wq	Write (save) and quit file
:w	Write (save) file
:w!	Write (save) file, overriding protection
:30,60w *newfile*	Write from line 30 through line 60 as *newfile*
:30,60w>> *file*	Write from line 30 through line 60 and append to *file*
:w %.new	Write current buffer named *file* as *file.new*
:q	Quit file
:q!	Quit file, overriding protection
Q	Quit *vi* and invoke *ex*
:e *file2*	Edit *file2* without leaving *vi*
:n	Edit next file
:e!	Return to version of current file at time of last write (save)
:e #	Edit alternate file
:vi	Invoke *vi* editor from *ex*
:	Invoke one *ex* command from *vi* editor

Command	Meaning
%	Current filename (substitutes into *ex* command line)
#	Alternate filename (substitutes into *ex* command line)

Solaris vi Command-Mode Tag Commands

Command	Action
^]	Look up the location of the identifier under the cursor in the *tags* file and move to that location; if tag stacking is enabled, the current location is automatically pushed onto the tag stack
^T	Return to the previous location in the tag stack, i.e., pop off one element

Buffer Names

Buffer Names	Buffer Use
1–9	The last nine deletions, from most to least recent
a–z	Named buffers to use as needed; uppercase letters append to the buffer

Buffer and Marking Commands

Command	Meaning
"*b command*	Do *command* with buffer *b*
m*x*	Mark current position with *x*
'*x*	Move cursor to first character of line marked by *x*

Command	Meaning
`x	Move cursor to character marked by x
` `	Return to exact position of previous mark or context
' '	Return to beginning of the line of previous mark or context

3. Input Mode Shortcuts

Word Abbreviation

:ab *abbr phrase*
>   Define *abbr* as an abbreviation for *phrase*.

:unab *abbr*
>   Remove definition of *abbr*.

Be careful with abbreviation texts that either end with the abbreviation name or contain the abbreviation name in the middle.

Command and Input Mode Maps

:map *x sequence*
>   Define character(s) *x* as a *sequence* of editing commands.

:unmap *x*
>   Disable the *sequence* defined for *x*.

:map
>   List the characters that are currently mapped.

:map! *x sequence*
>   Define character(s) *x* as a *sequence* of editing commands or text that will be recognized in input mode.

`:unmap! x`
> Disable the *sequence* defined for the input mode map *x*.

`:map!`
> List the characters that are currently mapped for interpretation in insert mode.

For both command and input mode maps, the map name *x* can take several forms:

One character
> When you type the character, *vi* executes the associated sequence of commands.

Multiple characters
> All the characters must be typed within one second. The value of `notimeout` changes the behavior.

`#n` Function key notation: a `#` followed by a digit *n* represents the sequence of characters sent by the terminal's function key number *n*.

To enter characters such as Escape (`^[`) or carriage return (`^M`), first type a CTRL-V (`^V`).

Executable Buffers

Named buffers provide yet another way to create "macros"—complex command sequences you can repeat with a few keystrokes. Here's how it's done:

1. Type a *vi* command sequence or an *ex* command *preceded by a colon*; return to command mode.

2. Delete the text into a named buffer.

3. Execute the buffer with the `@` command followed by the buffer letter.

The *ex* command :@*buf-name* works similarly.

Some versions treat * identically to @ when used from the *ex* command line. In addition, if the buffer character supplied after the @ or * commands is *, the command is taken from the default (unnamed) buffer.

Automatic Indentation

You enable automatic indentation with the command:

```
:set autoindent
```

Four special input sequences affect automatic indentation:

^T Add one level of indentation; typed in insert mode

^D Remove one level of indentation; typed in insert mode

^ ^D

 Shift the cursor back to the beginning of the line, but only for the current line*

0 ^D

 Shift the cursor back to the beginning of the line and reset the current auto-indent level to zero†

Two commands can be used for shifting source code:

<< Shift a line left eight spaces

>> Shift a line right eight spaces

The default shift is the value of **shiftwidth**, usually eight spaces.

---

* ^ ^D and 0 ^D are not in *elvis* 2.0.

† The *nvi* 1.79 documentation has these two commands switched, but the program actually behaves as described here.

---

4. Substitution and Regular Expressions

The Substitute Command

The general form of the substitute command is:

```
:[addr1[,addr2]]s/old/new/[flags]
```

Omitting the search pattern (`:s//replacement/`) uses the last search or substitution regular expression.

An empty replacement part (`:s/pattern//`) "replaces" the matched text with nothing, effectively deleting it from the line.

Substitution flags

Flag	Meaning
c	Confirm each substitution
g	Change all occurrences of *old* to *new* on each line (globally)
p	Print the line after the change is made

It's often useful to combine the substitute command with the *ex* global command, `:g`:

```
:g/Object Oriented/s//Buzzword compliant/g
```

vi Regular Expressions

.   Matches any *single* character except a newline. Remember that spaces are treated as characters.

*   Matches zero or more (as many as there are) of the single character that immediately precedes it.

The * can follow a metacharacter, such as . or a range in brackets.

^   When used at the start of a regular expression, ^ requires that the following regular expression be found at the beginning of the line. When not at the beginning of a regular expression, ^ stands for itself.

$ When used at the end of a regular expression, $ requires that the preceding regular expression be found at the end of the line. When not at the end of a regular expression, $ stands for itself.

\   Treats the following special character as an ordinary character. (Use \ \ to get a literal backslash.)

[ ]

Matches any *one* of the characters enclosed between the brackets. A range of consecutive characters can be specified by separating the first and last characters in the range with a hyphen.

You can include more than one range inside brackets and specify a mix of ranges and separate characters.

Most metacharacters lose their special meaning inside brackets, so you don't need to escape them if you want to use them as ordinary characters. Within brackets, the three metacharacters you still need to escape are \ -]. (The hyphen (-) acquires meaning as a range specifier; to use an actual hyphen, you can also place it as the first character inside the brackets.)

A caret (^) has special meaning only when it's the first character inside the brackets, but in this case, the meaning differs from that of the normal ^ metacharacter. As the first character within brackets, a ^ reverses their sense: the brackets match any one character *not* in the list. For example, `[^a-z]` matches any character that's not a lowercase letter.

`\(  \)`

Saves the pattern enclosed between `\(` and `\)` into a special holding space or "hold buffer." Up to nine patterns can be saved in this way on a single line.

You can also use the `\n` notation within a search or substitute string:

```
:s/\(abcd\)\1/alphabet-soup/
```

changes `abcdabcd` into `alphabet-soup`.*

`\<  \>`

Matches characters at the beginning (`\<`) or end (`\>`) of a word. The end or beginning of a word is determined either by a punctuation mark or by a space. Unlike `\(...\)`, these don't have to be used in matched pairs.

`~`   Matches whatever regular expression was used in the *last* search.

POSIX Bracket Expressions

POSIX bracket expressions may contain the following:

Character classes

A POSIX character class consists of keywords bracketed by `[:` and `:]`. The keywords describe different classes of characters such as alphabetic characters, control characters, and so on (see the following table).

---

* This works with *vi*, *nvi*, and *vim*, but not with *elvis* 2.0, *vile* 7.4, or *vile* 8.0.

Collating symbols

A collating symbol is a multicharacter sequence that should be treated as a unit. It consists of the characters bracketed by [. and .].

Equivalence classes

An equivalence class lists a set of characters that should be considered equivalent, such as e and è. It consists of a named element from the locale, bracketed by [= and =].

All three constructs must appear inside the square brackets of a bracket expression.

POSIX character classes

Class	Matching Characters
[:alnum:]	Alphanumeric characters
[:alpha:]	Alphabetic characters
[:blank:]	Space and tab characters
[:cntrl:]	Control characters
[:digit:]	Numeric characters
[:graph:]	Printable and visible (nonspace) characters
[:lower:]	Lowercase characters
[:print:]	Printable characters (includes whitespace)
[:punct:]	Punctuation characters
[:space:]	Whitespace characters
[:upper:]	Uppercase characters
[:xdigit:]	Hexadecimal digits

Metacharacters Used in Replacement Strings

\n Is replaced with the text matched by the *n*th pattern previously saved by \ (and \ ) , where *n* is a number from 1 to 9, and previously saved patterns (kept in hold buffers) are counted from the left on the line.

\   Treats the following special character as an ordinary character. To specify a real backslash, type two in a row (\ \ ).

&   Is replaced with the entire text matched by the search pattern when used in a replacement string. This is useful when you want to avoid retyping text.

~   The string found is replaced with the replacement text specified in the last substitute command. This is useful for repeating an edit.

\u or \l
: Changes the next character in the replacement string to upper- or lowercase, respectively.

\U or \L and \e or \E
: \U and \L are similar to \u or \l, but all following characters are converted to upper- or lowercase until the end of the replacement string or until \e or \E is reached. If there is no \e or \E, all characters of the replacement text are affected by the \U or \L.

More Substitution Tricks

- You can instruct *vi* to ignore case by typing :set ic.

- A simple :s is the same as :s//~/.

---

                 4. Substitution and Regular Expressions

- `:&` is the same as `:s`. You can follow the `&` with a `g` to make the substitution globally on the line, and even use it with a line range.

- The ⃞`&` key can be used as a *vi* command to perform the `:&` command, i.e., to repeat the last substitution.

- The `:~` command is similar to the `:&` command, but with a subtle difference. The search pattern used is the last regular expression used in *any* command, not necessarily the one used in the last substitute command.

- Besides the `/` character, you may use any nonalphanumeric, nonwhitespace character as your delimiter, except backslash, double-quote, and the vertical bar (`\`, `"`, and `|`).

- When the `edcompatible` option is enabled, *vi* remembers the flags (`g` for global and `c` for confirmation) used on the last substitute and applies them to the next one.

5. *ex Commands*

Command Syntax

` :[address] command [options]`

Address Symbols

Address	Includes
1,$	All lines in the file
x,y	Lines x through y
x;y	Lines x through y, with current line reset to x
0	Top of file
.	Current line

Address	Includes
n	Absolute line number *n*
$	Last line
%	All lines; same as 1,$
x-n	*n* lines before *x*
x+n	*n* lines after *x*
-[*n*]	One or *n* lines previous
+[*n*]	One or *n* lines ahead
'*x*	Line marked with *x*
''	Previous mark
/pat/ or ?pat?	Ahead or back to line where *pat* matches

Command Option Symbols

Symbol	Meaning
!	A variant form of the command
count	Repeat the command *count* times
file	Filename: % is current file, # is previous file

Alphabetical List of Commands

Full Name	Command
Abbrev	ab [*string text*]
Append	[*address*] a[!]
	text
	.
Args	ar
Change	[*address*] c[!]
	text
	.
Copy	[*address*] co *destination*

Full Name	Command
Delete	[*address*] d [*buffer*]
Edit	e [!][+n] [*filename*]
File	f [*filename*]
Global	[*address*]g[!]/*pattern*/[*commands*]
Insert	[*address*]i[!]
	text
	.
Join	[*address*]j[!][*count*]
K (mark)	[*address*] k *char*
List	[*address*] l [*count*]
Map	map *char commands*
Mark	[*address*] ma *char*
Move	[*address*] m *destination*
Next	n[!] [[+*command*] *filelist*]
Number	[*address*] nu [*count*]
Open	[*address*] o [/*pattern*/]
Preserve	pre
Print	[*address*] p [*count*]
	[*address*] P [*count*]
Put	[*address*] pu [*char*]
Quit	q[!]
Read	[*address*] r *filename*
Read	[*address*] r ! *command*
Recover	rec [*filename*]
Rewind	rew[!]
Set	set
	set *option*
	set no*option*
	set *option*=*value*
	set *option*?
Shell	sh
Source	so *filename*

Full Name	Command
Substitute	[addr] s [/pat/repl/] [opts]
T (to)	[address]t destination
Tag	[address] ta tag
Unabbreviate	una word
Undo	u
Unmap	unm char
V (global exclude)	[address] v/pattern/ [commands]
Version	ve
Visual	[address] vi [type] [count]
Visual	vi [+n] [filename]
Write	[address] w[!] [[>>]filename]
Write	[address] w !command
Wq (write + quit)	wq[!]
Xit	x
Yank	[address] y [char] [count]
Z (position line)	[address] z [type] [count]

type can be one of:

+   Place line at the top of the window (default)

–   Place line at bottom of the window

.   Place line in the center of the window

^   Print the previous window

=   Place line in the center of the window and leave the current line at this line

!	[address] !command
= (line number)	[address] =
< > (shift)	[address] < [count]
	[address] > [count]
Address	address

Full Name	Command
Return (next line)	RETURN
&	[address] & [options] [count] repeat substitute
~	[address]~[count] Like &, but with last used regular expression; for details, see Chapter 6 of *Learning the vi Editor*

6. Initialization and Recovery

Initialization

vi performs the following initialization steps:

1. If the EXINIT environment variable exists, execute the commands it contains. Separate multiple commands by a pipe symbol (|).

2. If EXINIT doesn't exist, look for the file *$HOME/.exrc*. If it exists, read and execute it.

3. If either EXINIT or *$HOME/.exrc* turns on the exrc option, read and execute the file *./.exrc*, if it exists.

4. Execute search or goto commands given with +/*pattern* or +*n* command-line options (POSIX: -c option).

The *.exrc* files are simple scripts of *ex* commands; they don't need a leading colon. You can put comments in your scripts by starting a line with a double quote ("). This is recommended.

Recovery

The commands ex -r or vi -r list any files you can recover. You then use the command:

```
$ vi -r file
```

to recover a particular *file*.

Even without a crash, you can force the system to preserve your buffer by using the command `:pre` (preserve).

7. *vi Options*

Option	Default
autoindent (ai)	noai
autoprint (ap)	ap
autowrite (aw)	noaw
beautify (bf)	nobf
directory (dir)	*/tmp*
edcompatible	noedcompatible
errorbells (eb)	errorbells
exrc (ex)	noexrc
hardtabs (ht)	8
ignorecase (ic)	noic
lisp	nolisp
list	nolist
magic	magic
mesg	mesg
novice	nonovice
number (nu)	nonu
open	open
optimize (opt)	noopt
paragraphs (para)	IPLPPPQP LIpplpipbp
prompt	prompt
readonly (ro)	noro
redraw (re)	

Option	Default
remap	remap
report	5
scroll	half window
sections (sect)	SHNHH HU
shell (sh)	*/bin/sh*
shiftwidth (sw)	8
showmatch (sm)	nosm
showmode	noshowmode
slowopen (slow)	
tabstop (ts)	8
taglength (tl)	0
tags	*tags /usr/lib/tags*
tagstack	tagstack
term	(from $TERM)
terse	noterse
timeout (to)	timeout
ttytype	(from $TERM)
warn	warn
window (w)	
wrapscan (ws)	ws
wrapmargin (wm)	0
writeany (wa)	nowa

8. *Enhanced Tags and Tag Stacks*

Exuberant ctags

The "Exuberant *ctags*" program was written by Darren Hiebert (home page: *http://home.hiwaay.net/~darren/ctags/*). As of this writing, the current version is 2.0.3.

This enhanced *tags* file format has three tab-separated fields: the tag name (typically an identifier), the source file containing the tag, and where to find the identifier. Extended attributes are placed after a separating `;"`. Each attribute is separated from the next by a tab character and consists of two colon-separated subfields. The first subfield is a keyword describing the attribute; the second is the actual value.

Extended ctags keywords

Keyword	Meaning
kind	The value is a single letter that indicates the lexical type of the tag
file	For static tags, i.e., local to the file
function	For local tags
struct	For fields in a struct
enum	For values in an enum data type
class	For C++ member functions and variables
scope	Intended mostly for C++ class member functions
arity	For functions

If the field doesn't contain a colon, it's assumed to be of type kind.

Within the value part of each attribute, the backslash, tab, carriage return, and newline characters should be encoded as \\, \t, \r, and \n, respectively.

Solaris 2.6 vi Tag Stacking

Tag commands

Command	Function
ta[g][!] *tagstring*	Edit the file containing *tagstring* as defined in the *tags* file
po[p][!]	Pop the tag stack by one element

Command-mode tag commands

Command	Function
^]	Look up the location of the identifier under the cursor in the *tags* file and move to that location; if tag stacking is enabled, the current location is automatically pushed onto the tag stack
^T	Return to the previous location in the tag stack, i.e., pop off one element

Options for tag management

Option	Function
taglength, tl	Controls the number of significant characters in a tag that is to be looked up; the default value of zero indicates that all characters are significant
tags, tagpath	The value is a list of filenames in which to look for tags, the default value is "tags /usr/lib/tags"
tagstack	When set to true, *vi* stacks each location on the tag stack

9. nvi — New vi

Important Command-Line Arguments

-c *command*
: Execute *command* at startup.

-F Don't copy the entire file when starting to edit.

-R Start in read-only mode, setting the **readonly** option.

-S Run with the **secure** option set, disallowing access to external programs.

-s Enter batch (script) mode. This is only for *ex* and is intended for running editing scripts. Prompts and non-error messages are disabled.

nvi Window Management Commands

Command	Function
bg	Hide the current window
di[splay] b[uffers]	Display all buffers, including named, unnamed, and numeric buffers
di[splay] s[creens]	Display the filenames of all backgrounded windows
Edit *filename*	Edit *filename* in a new window
Edit /tmp	Create a new window editing an empty buffer; */tmp* is interpreted especially to create a new temporary file
fg *filename*	Uncover *filename* into the current window
Fg *filename*	Uncover *filename* in a new window; the current window is split

Command	Function
Next	Edit the next file in the argument list in a new window
Previous	Edit the previous file in the argument list in a new window
resize +*nrows*	Increase or decrease the size of the current window by *nrows* rows
Tag *tagstring*	Edit the file containing *tagstring* in a new window

The ^W command cycles between windows, top to bottom. The :q and ZZ commands exit the current window.

You may have multiple windows open in the same file. Changes made in one window are reflected in the other.

Extended Regular Expressions

You use :set extended to enable extended regular expression matching:

| Indicates alternation. The left and right sides don't need to be single characters.

(...)
    Used for grouping, to allow the application of additional regular expression operators.

ı   Matches one or more of the preceding regular expressions. This is either a single character or a group of characters enclosed in parentheses.

?   Matches zero or one occurrence of the preceding regular expression.

{...}

> Defines an *interval expression*. Interval expressions describe counted numbers of repetitions. In the following description, *n* and *m* represent integer constants:
>
> {*n*}
>
>> Matches exactly *n* repetitions of the previous regular expression.
>
> {*n*,}
>
>> Matches *n* or more repetitions of the previous regular expression.
>
> {*n*,*m*}
>> Matches *n* to *m* repetitions.

When **extended** isn't set, use \{ and \}.

When **extended** is set, you should precede the above metacharacters with a backslash in order to match them literally.

Command-Line History and Completion Options

Option	Description
cedit	The first character of this string, when used on the colon command line, provides access to the command history; hitting RETURN on any given line executes that line
filec	The first character of this string, when used on the colon command line, does shell-style filename expansion; when this character is the same as for the cedit option, command-line editing is performed only when the character is entered as the first character on the colon command line

Tag Stacks

Tag commands

Command	Function
di[splay] t[ags]	Display the tag stack
ta[g][!] *tagstring*	Edit the file containing *tagstring* as defined in the *tags* file
Ta[g][!] *tagstring*	Just like :tag, except that the file is edited in a new window
tagp[op][!] *tagloc*	Pop to the given tag, or to the most recently used tag if no *tagloc* is supplied
tagt[op][!]	Pop to the oldest tag in the stack, clearing the stack in the process

Command-mode tag commands

Command	Function
^]	Look up the location of the identifier under the cursor in the *tags* file and move to that location; the current location is automatically pushed to the tag stack
^T	Return to the previous location in the tag stack

nvi 1.79 Additional Set Options

Option	Default
backup	
cdpath	Environment variable $CDPATH, or current directory
cedit	
comment	nocomment

Option	Default
directory (dir)	$TMPDIR, or */tmp*
extended	noextended
filec	
iclower	noiclower
leftright	noleftright
lock	lock
octal	nooctal
path	
recdir	*/var/tmp/vi.recover*
ruler	noruler
searchincr	nosearchincr
secure	nosecure
shellmeta	~{[*?$`'"\
showmode (smd)	noshowmode
sidescroll	16
taglength (tl)	0
tags (tag)	*tags /var/db/libc.tags /sys/kern/tags*
tildeop	notildeop
wraplen (wl)	0

10. elvis

Important Command-Line Arguments

-a Load each file named on the command line to a separate window.

-R Start editing each file in read-only mode.

-i Start editing in input mode instead of in command mode.

-s Set the **safer** option for the whole session, not just execution of *.exrc* files. In *elvis* 2.1, this option is renamed to -S, and (following the POSIX standard) -s provides *ex* scripting.

-f *filename*
   Use *filename* for the session file instead of the default name.

-G *gui*
   Use the given interface.

-c *command*
   Execute *command* at startup (POSIX version of the historic +*command* syntax).

-V Output more verbose status information.

-? Print a summary of the possible options.

elvis Window Management Commands

Command	Function
sp[lit] [*file*]	Create a new window; load it with *file* if supplied; otherwise, the new window shows the current file
new sne[w]	Create a new empty buffer and then create a new window to show that buffer
sn[ext] [*file*...]	Create a new window, showing the next *file* in the argument list
sN[ext]	Create a new window, showing the previous file in the argument list
sre[wind][!]	Create a new window, showing the first file in the argument list; reset the "current" file as the first with respect to the :next command

Command	Function
sl[ast]	Create a new window, showing the last file in the argument list
sta[g][!] tag	Create a new window showing the file where the requested tag is found
sa[ll]	Create a new window for any files named in the argument list that don't already have a window
wi[ndow] [target]	With no target, list all windows; the possible values for target are described in the following table
close	Close the current window; the buffer that the window was displaying remains intact
wquit	Write the buffer back to the file and close the window; the file is saved whether or not it has been modified
qall	Issue a :q command for each window; buffers without windows are not affected

Arguments to the :window command

Argument	Meaning
+	Switch to the next window, like ^W k
++	Switch to the next window, wrapping like ^W ^W
–	Switch to the previous window, like ^W j
– –	Switch to the previous window, wrapping
num	Switch to the window whose windowid =num
buffer-name	Switch to the window editing the named buffer

Window commands from vi command mode

Command	Function
^W c	Hide the buffer and close the window
^W d	Toggle the display mode between "normal" and the buffer's usual display mode; this is a per-window option
^W j	Move down to the next window
^W k	Move up to the previous window
^W n	Create a new window and a new buffer to be displayed in the window
^W q	Save the buffer and close the window
^W s	Split the current window
^W S	Toggle the **wrap** option; this option controls whether long lines wrap or whether the whole screen scrolls to the right, and is a per-window option
^W]	Create a new window, then look up the tag underneath the cursor
[*count*] ^W ^W	Move to next window, or to the *count*th window
^W +	Increase the size of the current window (*termcap* interface only)
^W −	Reduce the size of the current window (*termcap* interface only)
^W \	Make the current window as large as possible (*termcap* interface only)

Extended Regular Expressions

\+ Matches one or more of the preceding regular expressions

\?   Matches zero or one of the preceding regular expressions

\@   Matches the word under the cursor

\=   Indicates where to put the cursor when the text is matched

\{...\}
    Describes an interval expression

POSIX bracket expressions (character classes, etc.) don't work in *elvis* 2.0 (fixed in 2.1), nor is alternation with the | character or grouping with parentheses available.

Command-Line History and Completion Movement Keys

Key	Effect
↑, ↓	Page up and down through the Elvis ex history buffer
←, →	Move around on the command line

Insert characters by typing and erase them by backspacing over them.

The ⌈TAB⌋ key can be used for filename expansion.

To get a real tab character, precede it with a ^V. Disable filename completion entirely by setting the Elvis ex history buffer's **inputtab** option to **tab**, via the following command:

```
:(Elvis ex history)set inputtab=tab
```

Tag Stacks

Tag commands

Command	Function
ta[g][!] [*tagstring*]	Edit the file containing *tagstring* as defined in the *tags* file
stac[k]	Display the current tag stack
po[p][!]	Pop a cursor position off the stack, restoring the cursor to its previous position

Command-mode tag commands

Command	Function
^]	Look up the location of the identifier under the cursor in the *tags* file and move to that location; the current location is automatically pushed onto the tag stack
^T	Return to the previous location in the tag stack

Edit-Compile Speedup

Program development commands

Command	Option	Function
cc[l] [*args*]	ccprg	Run the C compiler; useful for recompiling an individual file
mak[e][!] [*args*]	makeprg	Recompile everything that needs recompiling (usually via *make*(1))

Command	Option	Function
er[rlist][!] [*file*]		Move to the next error's location

Display modes

Mode	Display Appearance
normal	No formatting; display text as it exists in the file
syntax	Like normal, but with syntax coloring turned on
hex	An interactive hex dump, reminiscent of main-frame hex dumps; good for editing binary files
html	A simple web page formatter; the tag commands can follow links and return
man	Simple manpage formatter; like the output of nroff -man

Display-mode commands

Command	Function
di[splay] [*mode* [*lang*]]	Change the display mode to *mode*; use *lang* for syntax mode
no[rmal]	Same as :display normal, but much easier to type

Options for print management

Option	Function
lptype, lp	The printer type
lpconvert, lpcvt	If set, convert Latin-8 extended ASCII to PC-8 extended ASCII

Option	Function
lpcrlf, lpc	The printer needs CR-LF to end each line
lpout, lpo	The file or command to print to
lpcolumns, lpcols	The printer's width
lpwrap, lpw	Simulate line wrapping
lplines, lprows	The length of the printer's page
lpformfeed, lpff	Send a formfeed after the last page
lppaper, lpp	Size of the paper (letter, A4, etc.); only for PostScript printers

Values for the lptype option

Name	Printer Type
ps	PostScript; one logical page per sheet of paper
ps2	PostScript; two logical pages per sheet of paper
epson	Most dot-matrix printers; no graphic characters supported
pana	Panasonic dot-matrix printers
ibm	Dot-matrix printers with IBM graphic characters
hp	Hewlett-Packard printers and most non-PostScript laser printers
cr	Line printers; overtyping is done with carriage return
bs	Overtyping is done via backspace characters; this setting is the closest to traditional Unix *nroff*
dumb	Plain ASCII; no font control

elvis 2.0 Set Options

Option	Default
autoiconify (aic)	noautoiconify
backup (bk)	nobackup
binary (bin)	(Set automatically)
boldfont (xfb)	
bufdisplay (bd)	normal
ccprg (cp)	cc ($1?$1:$2)
commentfont (cfont)	
directory (dir)	
display (mode)	normal
elvispath (epath)	(System dependent)
focusnew (fn)	focusnew
functionfont (ffont)	
gdefault (gd)	nogdefault
home (home)	$HOME
italicfont (xfi)	
keywordfont (kfont)	
lpcolumns (lpcols)	80
lpcrlf (lpc)	nolpcrlf
lpformfeed (lpff)	nolpformfeed
lplines (lprows)	60
lppaper (lpp)	letter
lpout (lpo)	
lptype (lpt)	dumb
lpwrap (lpw)	lpwrap
makeprg (mp)	make $1
normalfont (xfn)	
otherfont (ofont)	
prepfont (pfont)	
ruler (ru)	noruler

Option	Default
safer (trapunsafe)	nosafer
showmarkups (smu)	noshowmarkups
sidescroll (ss)	0
stringfont (sfont)	
taglength (tl)	0
tags (tagpath)	*tags*
tagstack (tsk)	tagstack
undolevels (ul)	0
variablefont (vfont)	
warpback (wb)	nowarpback
warpto (wt)	don't

11. vim — vi Improved

Important Command-Line Arguments

-c *command*
> Execute *command* at startup. (POSIX version of the historic *+command*)

-R Start in read-only mode, setting the readonly option.

-s Enter batch (script) mode. This is only for *ex* and intended for running editing scripts (POSIX version of the historic "–" argument).

-b Start in binary mode.

-f For the GUI version, stay in the foreground.

-g Start the GUI version of *vim*, if it has been compiled in.

-o [*N*]

    Open *N* windows, if given; otherwise open one window per file.

-i *viminfo*

    Read the given *viminfo* file for initialization, instead of the default *viminfo* file.

-n Don't create a swap file: recovery won't be possible.

-q *filename*

    Treat *filename* as the "quick fix" file.

-u *vimrc*

    Read the given *.vimrc* file for initialization and skip all other normal initialization steps.

-U *gvimrc*

    Read the given *.gvimrc* file for GUI initialization and skip all other normal GUI initialization steps.

-Z Enter restricted mode (same as having a leading *r* in the name).

vim Window Management Commands

Command	Function
[*N*]sp[lit] [*position*] [*file*]	Split the current window in half
[*N*]new [*position*] [*file*]	Create a new window, editing an empty buffer
[*N*]sv[iew] [*position*] [*file*]	Same as :split, but set the readonly option for the buffer
q[uit][!]	Quit the current window (exit if given in the last window)

Command	Function
clo[se][!]	Close the current window; behavior affected by the `hidden` option
hid[e]	Close the current window, if it's not the last one on the screen
on[ly]	Make this window the only one on the screen
res[ize] [±n]	Increase or decrease the current window height by *n*
res[ize] [n]	Set the current window height to *n* if supplied, otherwise, set it to the largest size possible without hiding the other windows
qa[ll][!]	Exit *vim*
wqa[ll][!] xa[ll][!]	Write all changed buffers and exit
wa[ll][!]	Write all modified buffers that have filenames
[N]sn[ext]	Split the window and move to the next file in the argument list, or to the *N*th file if a count is supplied
sta[g] [tagname]	Split the window and run the `:tag` command as appropriate in the new window

Window commands from vi mode

Command	Function
^W s ^W S ^W ^S	Same as :split without a *file* argument; ^W ^S may not work on all terminals
^W n ^W ^N	Same as :new without a *file* argument
^W ^ ^W ^^	Perform :split #, split the window, and edit the alternate file
^W q ^W ^Q	Same as the :quit command; ^W ^Q may not work on all terminals
^W c	Same as the :close command
^W o ^W ^O	Like the :only command
^W <DOWN> ^W j ^W ^J	Move cursor to *n*th window below the current one
^W <UP> ^W k ^W ^K	Move cursor to *n*th window above the current one
^W w ^W ^W	With *count*, go to *n*th window; otherwise, move to the window below the current one; if in the bottom window, move to the top one
^W W	With *count*, go to *n*th window; otherwise, move to window above the current one; if in the top window, move to the bottom one
^W t ^W ^T	Move the cursor to the top window

Command	Function
^W b ^W ^B	Move the cursor to the bottom window
^W p ^W ^P	Go to the most recently accessed (previous) window
^W r ^W ^R	Rotate all the windows downwards; the cursor stays in the same window
^W R	Rotate all the windows upwards; the cursor stays in the same window
^W x ^W ^X	Without *count*, exchange the current window with the next one; if there is no next window, exchange with the previous window. With *count*, exchange the current window with the *n*th window (first window is 1; the cursor is put in the other window)
^W =	Make all windows the same height.
^W –	Decrease current window height
^W +	Increase current window height
^W _ ^W ^_	Set the current window size to the value given in a preceding count
z*N* RETURN	Set the current window height to *N*
^W] ^W ^]	Split the current window; in the new upper window, use the identifier under the cursor as a tag and go to it
^W f ^W ^F	Split the current window and edit the filename under the cursor in the new window
^W i ^W ^I	Open a new window; move the cursor to the first line that matches the keyword under the cursor

Command	Function
^W d ^W ^D	Open a new window, with the cursor on the first macro definition line that contains the keyword under the cursor

Extended Regular Expressions

\| Indicates alternation.

\+ Matches one or more of the preceding regular expressions.

\= Matches zero or one of the preceding regular expression.

\{n,m}

  Matches *n* to *m* of the preceding regular expression, as much as possible. *n* and *m* are numbers between 0 and 32,000; *vim* only requires the left brace to be preceded by a backslash, but not the right brace.

\{n}

  Matches *n* of the preceding regular expression.

\{n, }

  Matches at least *n* of the preceding regular expression, as much as possible.

\{,m}

  Matches 0 to *m* of the preceding regular expression, as much as possible.

\{}

  Matches 0 or more of the preceding regular expressions, as much as possible (same as *).

\{-n,m}

  Matches *n* to *m* of the preceding regular expression, as few as possible.

`\{-n}`

   Matches *n* of the preceding regular expression.

`\{-n,}`

   Matches at least *n* of the preceding regular expression, as few as possible.

`\{-,m}`

   Matches 0 to *m* of the preceding regular expression, as few as possible.

`\i` Matches any identifier character, as defined by the `isident` option.

`\I` Like `\i`, excluding digits.

`\k` Matches any keyword character, as defined by the `iskeyword` option.

`\K` Like `\k`, excluding digits.

`\f` Matches any filename character, as defined by the `isfname` option.

`\F` Like `\f`, excluding digits.

`\p` Matches any printable character, as defined by the `isprint` option.

`\P` Like `\p`, excluding digits.

`\s` Matches a whitespace character (exactly space or tab).

`\S` Matches anything that isn't a space or a tab.

`\b` Backspace.

`\e` Escape.

`\r` Carriage return.

\t Tab.

\n Reserved for future use.

~ Matches the last given substitute (i.e., replacement) string.

\ (... \ )
Provides grouping for *, \+, and \=, as well as making matched subtexts available in the replacement part of a substitute command (\1, \2, etc.).

\1 Matches the same string that was matched by the first subexpression in \ (and \). \2, \3 and so on may be used to represent the second, third, and so forth subexpressions.

The isident, iskeyword, isfname, and isprint options define the characters that appear in identifiers, keywords, and filenames, and that are printable, respectively.

Command-Line History and Completion

History commands

Key	Meaning
↑, ↓	Move up (previous), down (more recent) in the history
←, →	Move left, right on the recalled line
INS	Toggle insert/overstrike mode; default is insert mode
BACKSPACE	Delete characters
SHIFT or CONTROL combined with ← or →	Move left or right one word at a time
^B or HOME	Move to the beginning of the command line

Key	Meaning
^E or END	Move to the end of the command line

If *vim* is in *vi* compatibility mode, ESC acts likes RETURN and executes the command. When *vi* compatibility is turned off, ESC exits the command line without executing anything.

The `wildchar` option contains the character you type when you want *vim* to do a completion. The default value is the tab character. You can use completion for the following:

Command names
: Available at the start of the command line

Tag values
: After you've typed `:tag`

Filenames
: When typing a command that takes a filename argument (see `:help suffixes` for details)

Option values
: When entering a `:set` command, for both option names and their values

Completion commands

Command	Function
^D	List the names that match the pattern; for filenames, directories are high-lighted
Value of `wildchar`	(Default: tab) Performs a match, inserting the generated text; hitting TAB successively cycles among all the matches

Command	Function
^N	Go to next of multiple `wildchar` matches, if any; otherwise recall more recent history line
^P	Go to previous of multiple `wildchar` matches, if any; otherwise recall older history line
^A	Insert all names that match the pattern
^L	If there is exactly one match, insert it; otherwise, expand to the longest common prefix of the multiple matches

Tag Stacks

Tag commands

Command	Function
ta[g][!] [*tagstring*]	Edit the file containing *tagstring* as defined in the *tags* file
[*count*]ta[g][!]	Jump to the *count*th newer entry in the tag stack
[*count*]po[p][!]	Pop a cursor position off the stack, restoring the cursor to its previous position
tags	Display the contents of the tag stack
ts[elect][!] [*tagstring*]	List the tags that match *tagstring*, using the information in the tags file(s)
sts[elect][!] [*tagstring*]	Like :tselect, but splits the window for the selected tag
[*count*]tn[ext][!]	Jump to the *count*th next matching tag (default 1)

Command	Function
[count]tp[revious][!] [count]tN[ext][!]	Jump to the countth previous matching tag (default 1)
[count]tr[ewind][!]	Jump to the first matching tag; with count, jump to the countth matching tag
tl[ast][!]	Jump to the last matching tag

Command-mode tag commands

Command	Function
^] g \<LeftMouse\> CTRL-\<LeftMouse\>	Look up the location of the identifier under the cursor in the *tags* file and move to that location; the current location is automatically pushed to the tag stack
^T	Return to the previous location in the tag stack, i.e., pop off one element

Edit-Compile Speedup

Program development commands

Command	Function
mak[e] [arguments]	Run *make*, based on the settings of several options as described in the next table, then go to the location of the first error
cf[ile][!] [errorfile]	Read the error file and jump to the first error
cl[ist][!]	List the errors that include a filename

Command	Function
[*count*]cn[ext][!]	Display the *count*th next error that includes a filename
[*count*]cN[ext][!] [*count*]cp[revious][!]	Display the *count*th previous error that includes a filename
clast[!] [*n*]	Display error *n* if supplied; otherwise, display the last error
crewind[!] [*n*]	Display error *n* if supplied
cc[!] [*n*]	Displays error *n* if supplied, otherwise redisplays the current error
cq[uit]	Quit with an error code, so that the compiler won't compile the same file again; intended primarily for the Amiga compiler

Program development options

Option	Value	Function
shell	/bin/sh	The shell to execute the command for rebuilding your program
makeprg	make	The program that actually handles the recompilation
shellpipe	2>&1 | tee	Whatever is needed to cause the shell to save both standard output and standard error from the compilation in the error file

Option	Value	Function
makeef	/tmp/vim##.err	The name of a file that will contain the compiler output; the ## causes *vim* to create unique filenames
errorformat	%f:%l:\ %m	A description of what error messages from the compiler look like; this example value is for GCC, the GNU C compiler

Programming Assistance

Indentation and formatting options

Option	Function
autoindent	Simple-minded indentation; uses that of the previous line
smartindent	Similar to autoindent, but knows a little about C syntax; deprecated in favor of cindent
cindent	Enables automatic indenting for C programs and is quite smart; C formatting is affected by the rest of the options in this table
cinkeys	Input keys that trigger indentation options
cinoptions	Tailor your preferred indentation style
cinwords	Keywords that start an extra indentation on the following line
formatoptions	A number of single-letter flags that control several behaviors, notably how comments are formatted as you type them

Option	Function
comments	Describes different formatting options for different kinds of comments, both those with starting and ending delimiters, as in C, and those that start with a single symbol and go to the end of the line, such as in a *Makefile* or shell program

Identifier search commands

Command	Function
[i	Display the first line that contains the keyword under the cursor
]i	Display the first line that contains the keyword under the cursor, but starts the search at the current position in the file; this command is most effective when given a count
[I	Display all lines that contain the keyword under the cursor; filenames and line numbers are displayed
]I	Display all lines that contain the keyword under the cursor, but start from the current position in the file
[^I	Jump to the first occurrence of the keyword under the cursor
] ^I	Jump to the first occurrence of the keyword under the cursor, but start the search from the current position
^W i ^W ^I	Open a new window showing the location of the first (or *count*th) occurrence of the identifier under the cursor
[d	Display the first macro definition for the identifier under the cursor

Command	Function
]d	Display the first macro definition for the identifier under the cursor, but start the search from the current position
[D	Display all macro definitions for the identifier under the cursor; filenames and line numbers are displayed
]D	Display all macro definitions for the identifier under the cursor, but start the search from the current positon
[^D	Jump to the first macro definition for the identifier under the cursor
] ^D	Jump to the first macro definition for the identifier under the cursor, but start the search from the current position
^W d ^W ^D	Open a new window showing the location of the first (or *count*th) macro definition of the identifier under the cursor

Identifier search commands from ex mode

Command	Function
[*range*]is[earch][!] [*count*] [/]*pattern*[/]	Like [i and]i but searches in *range* lines (the default is the whole file). Without the slashes, a word search is done; with slashes, a regular expression search is done
[*range*]il[ist][!] [/]*pattern*[/]	Like [I and]I but searches in *range* lines; the default is the whole file
[*range*]ij[ump][!] [*count*] [/]*pattern*[/]	Like [^I and] ^I but searches in *range* lines; the default is the whole file

Command	Function
[range]isp[lit][!] [count] [/]pattern[/]	Like ^W i and ^W ^I but searches in *range* lines; the default is the whole file
[range]ds[earch][!] [count] [/]pattern[/]	Like [d and]d but searches in *range* lines; the default is the whole file
[range]dl[ist][!] [/]pattern[/]	Like [D and]D but searches in *range* lines; the default is the whole file
[range]dj[ump][!] [count] [/]pattern[/]	Like [^D and] ^D but searches in *range* lines. The default is the whole file.
[range]dsp[lit][!] [count] [/]pattern[/]	Like ^W d and ^W ^D but searches in *range* lines; the default is the whole file
che[ckpath][!]	List all the included files that couldn't be found; with the !, list all the included files

Extended matching commands

Command	Function
%	Extended to match the /* and */ of C comments, and also the C preprocessor conditionals, (#if, #endif, etc.)
[(	Move to the *count*th previous unmatched (
[ )	Move to the *count*th next unmatched)
[{	Move to the *count*th previous unmatched {
[}	Move to the *count*th next unmatched }
[#	Move to the *count*th previous unmatched #if or #else
] #	Move to the *count*th next unmatched #else or #endif

Command	Function
[*, [/	Move to the *count*th previous unmatched start of a C comment, /*
]*,]/	Move to the *count*th next unmatched end of a C comment, */

vim 5.1 Set Options

Option	Default
background (bg)	dark or light
backspace (bs)	0
backup (bk)	nobackup
backupdir (bdir)	., ~/tmp/, ~/
backupext (bex)	~
binary (bin)	nobinary
cindent (cin)	nocindent
cinkeys (cink)	0{,0},:,0#,!^F,o,O,e
cinoptions (cino)	
cinwords (cinw)	if,else,while,do,for,switch
comments (com)	
compatible (cp)	cp, nocp when a *.vimrc* file is found
cpoptions (cpo)	aABceFs
define (def)	^#\s*define
directory (dir)	., ~/tmp,/tmp
equalprg (ep)	
errorfile (ef)	errors.err
errorformat (efm)	(Too long to print)
expandtab (et)	noexpandtab
fileformat (ff)	unix

Option	Default
fileformats (ffs)	dos,unix
formatoptions (fo)	*vim* default: tcq; *vi* default: vt
gdefault (gd)	nogdefault
guifont (gfn)	
hidden (hid)	nohidden
hlsearch (hls)	nohlsearch
history (hi)	*vim* default: 20; *vi* default: 0
icon	noicon
iconstring	
include (inc)	^#\s*include
incsearch (is)	noincsearch
isfname (isf)	@,48-57,/,.,-,_,+,,,$,:,~
isident (isi)	@,48-57,_,192-255
iskeyword (isk)	@,48-57,_,192-255
isprint (isp)	@,161-255
makeef (mef)	*/tmp/vim##.err*
makeprg (mp)	make
mouse	
mousehide (mh)	nomousehide
paste	nopaste
ruler (ru)	noruler
secure	nosecure
shellpipe (sp)	
shellredir (srr)	
showmode (smd)	*vim* default: smd; *vi* default: nosmd
sidescroll (ss)	0
smartcase (scs)	nosmartcase
suffixes	*.bak,~,.o,.h,.info,.swp
taglength (tl)	0

Option	Default
tagrelative (tr)	*vim* default: tr; *vi* default: notr
tags (tag)	./tags,tags
tildeop (top)	notildeop
undolevels (ul)	1000
viminfo (vi)	
writebackup (wb)	writebackup

12. *vile*—*vi Like Emacs*

Important Command-Line Arguments

-? *vile* prints a short usage summary and exits.

-g *N*

> *vile* begins editing on the first file at the specified line number; this can also be given as +*N*.

-s *pattern*

> In the first file, *vile* executes an initial search for the given pattern; this can also be given as +/*pattern*.

-h Invokes *vile* on the help file.

-R Invokes *vile* in "readonly" mode; no writes are permitted while in this mode.

-v Invokes *vile* in "view" mode; no changes are permitted to any buffer while in this mode.

@*cmdfile*

> *vile* runs the specified file as its startup file and bypasses any normal startup file.

vile Window Management Commands

Command	Key Sequence(s)	Function
delete-other-windows	^O, ^X 1	Eliminate all windows except the current one
delete-window	^K, ^X 0	Destroy the current window, unless it's the last one
edit-file, E, e find-file	^X e	Bring given (or under-cursor, for ^X e) file or existing buffer into window
grow-window	V	Increase the size of the current window by *count*
move-next-window-down	^A ^E	Move next window down (or buffer up) by *count* lines
move-next-window-up	^A ^Y	Move next window up (or buffer down) by *count* lines
move-window-left	^X ^L	Scroll window to left by *count* columns, half screen if *count* unspecified
move-window-right	^X ^R	Scroll window to right by *count* columns, half screen if *count* unspecified
next-window	^X o	Move to the next window

Command	Key Sequence(s)	Function
position-window	z *where*	Reframe with cursor specified by *where*, as follows: center (., M, m), top (RETURN , H, t), or bottom (-, L, b)
previous-window	^X O	Move to the previous window
resize-window		Change the current window to *count* lines
restore-window		Return to window saved with save-window
save-window		Mark a window for later return with restore-window
scroll-next-window-down	^A ^D	Move next window down by *count* half screens
scroll-next-window-up	^A ^U	Move next window up by *count* half screens
shrink-window	v	Decrease the size of the current window by *count* lines
split-current-window	^X 2	Split the window in half; a *count* of 1 or 2 chooses which becomes current
view-file		Bring given file or existing buffer into window; mark it "view-only"

Command	Key Sequence(s)	Function
`historical-buffer`	_	Display a list of the first nine buffers; a digit moves to the given buffer, _ _ moves to the most recently edited file
`toggle-buffer-list`	*	Pop up/down a window showing all the *vile* buffers

Extended Regular Expressions

\| Indicates alternation.

\+ Matches one or more of the preceding regular expressions.

\? Matches zero or one of the preceding regular expression.

\(...\)
   Provides grouping for *, \+, and \?, as well as making matched subtexts available in the replacement part of a substitute command.

\s \S
   Matches whitespace and nonwhitespace characters, respectively.

\w \W
   Matches "word-constituent" characters (alphanumerics and the underscore, '_') and nonword-constituent characters, respectively.

\d \D
   Matches digits and nondigits, respectively.

`\p \P`

> Matches printable and nonprintable characters, respectively. Whitespace is considered to be printable.

vile allows the escape sequences `\b`, `\f`, `\r`, `\t`, and `\n`, to appear in the replacement part of a substitute command. They stand for backspace, formfeed, carriage return, tab, and newline, respectively. Also, from the *vile* documentation:

> Note that *vile* mimics *perl*'s handling of `\u\L\1\E` instead of *vi*'s. Given `:s/\(abc\)/\u\L\1\E/`, *vi* will replace with abc whereas *vile* and *perl* will replace with Abc. This is somewhat more useful for capitalizing words.

Command-Line History and Completion

vile stores all your *ex* commands in a buffer named [History]. Options control your access to it and the use of the minibuffer (the colon command line).

History options

Option	Meaning
history	Log commands from the colon command line in the [History] buffer
mini-edit	The character that toggles the editing mode in the minibuffer to use *vi* motion commands; in Version 8.0, you can also use the i, I, a, and A *vi* commands

Option	Meaning
mini-hilite	Define the highlight attribute to use when the user toggles the editing mode in the minibuffer. The value should be one of none, underline, bold, italic, or reverse; the default is reverse

History commands

Key	Meaning
↑, ↓	Move up (previous), down (more recent) in the history
←, →	Move left, right on the recalled line
BACKSPACE	Delete characters

The *ex* command line provides completion of various sorts. Completion applies to built-in and user-defined *vile* commands, tags, filenames, modes, variables, and to the terminal characters (the character setting such as backspace, suspend, and so on, derived from your *stty* settings).

Tag Stacks

Tag commands

Command	Function
ta[g][!] [*tagstring*]	Edit the file containing *tagstring* as defined in the *tags* file
pop[!]	Pop a cursor position off the stack, restoring the cursor to its previous position
next-tag	Continue searching through the *tags* file for more matches

Command	Function
show-tagstack	Create a new window that displays the tag stack; the display changes as tags are pushed to or popped off the stack

Command mode tag commands

Command	Function
^]	Look up the location of the identifier under the cursor in the *tags* file and move to that location; the current location is automatically pushed to the tag stack
^T ^X ^]	Return to the previous location in the tag stack, i.e., pop off one element
^A ^]	Same as the :next-tag command

Edit-Compile Speedup

Program development vi mode commands

Command	Function
^X !command RETURN	Run *command*, saving the output in a buffer named [Output]
^X ^X	Find the next error; *vile* parses the output and moves to the location of each successive error

The error messages are parsed using regular expressions in the buffer [Error Expressions]. *vile* creates this buffer automatically and uses it when you use ^X ^X. You can add expressions to it as needed.

You can point the error finder at an arbitrary buffer (not just the output of shell commands) using the `:error-buffer` command. This lets you use the error finder on the output of previous compiler or *egrep* runs.

vile 8.0 Set Options

Option	Default
alt-tabpos	noatp
animated	animated
autobuffer (ab)	autobuffer
autosave (as)	noautosave
autosavecnt (ascnt)	256
backspacelimit (bl)	backspacelimit
backup-style	off
bcolor	
check-modtime	nocheck-modtime
cmode	off
comment-prefix	^\s*\(\s*[#*>]\)\+
comments	^\s*/\?\(\s*[#*>]\)\+/\?\s*$
dirc	nodirc
dos	nodos
fcolor	
fence-begin	/*
fence-end	*/
fence-if	^\s*#\s*if
fence-elif	^\s*#\s*elif\>
fence-else	^\s*#\s*else\>
fence-fi	^\s*#\s*endif\>
fence-pairs	{}()[]
glob	!echo %s

Option	Default
history (hi)	history
horizscroll (hs)	horizscroll
linewrap (lw)	nolinewrap
maplonger	nomaplonger
meta-insert-bindings (mib)	nomib
mini-edit	^G
mini-hilite (mh)	reverse
popup-choices (pc)	delayed
preamble (pre)	
resolve-links	noresolve-links
ruler	noruler
showmode (smd)	noshowmode
sideways	0
suffixes (suf)	
tabinsert (ti)	tabinsert
tagignorecase (tc)	notagignorecase
taglength (tl)	0
tagrelative (tr)	tagrelative
tags	*tags*
tagword (tw)	notagword
undolimit (ul)	10
unprintable-as-octal (uo)	nounprintable-as-octal
visual-matches	none
xterm-mouse	noxterm-mouse

13. Clone Source and Contact Information

Editor	*nvi*
Author	Keith Bostic
Email	*bostic@bostic.com*
Source	*http://www.bostic.com/vi*
Editor	*elvis*
Author	Steve Kirkendall
Email	*kirkenda@cs.pdx.edu*
Source	*ftp://ftp.cs.pdx.edu/pub/elvis/README.html*
Editor	*vim*
Author	Bram Moolenaar
Email	*Bram@vim.org*
Source	*http://www.vim.org/*
Editor	*vile*
Authors	Kevin Buettner, Tom Dickey, and Paul Fox
Email	*vile-bugs@foxharp.boston.ma.us*
Source	*http://www.clark.net/pub/dickey/vile/vile.html*

Other Titles Available from O'Reilly

**Learning the UNIX Operating System,
5th Edition**

*By Jerry Peek, Grace Todino &
John Strang*
5th Edition November 2001
176 pages, ISBN 0-596-00261-0

Learning the UNIX Operating System
is the most effective introduction to
Unix in print. The fifth edition covers Internet usage for email, file
transfers, and web browsing. It's per-
fect for those who are just starting
with Unix or Linux, as well as any-
one who encounters a Unix system
on the Internet. Complete with a
quick-reference card to pull out and
keep handy, it's an ideal primer for
Mac and PC users of the Internet
who need to know a little bit about
Unix on the systems they visit.

Learning the Korn Shell, 2nd Edition

By Bill Rosenblatt, Arnold Robbins
2nd Edition April 2002
432 pages, ISBN 0-596-00195-9

Learning the Korn Shell is the key to
gaining control of the Korn shell and
becoming adept at using it as an
interactive command and scripting
language. Readers will learn how to
write many applications more easily
and quickly than with other high-
level languages. A solid offering for
many years, this newly revised title
inherits a long tradition of trust
among computer professionals who
want to learn or refine an essential
skill.

**UNIX in a Nutshell: System V Edition,
3rd Edition**

By Arnold Robbins
3rd Edition September 1999
616 pages, ISBN 1-56592-427-4

The bestselling, most informative
Unix reference book is now more
complete and up-to-date. Not a
scaled-down quick reference of com-
mon commands, *UNIX in a Nutshell*
is a complete reference containing all
commands and options, with
descriptions and examples that put
the commands in context. For all but
the thorniest Unix problems, this
one reference should be all you need.
Covers System V Release 4 and
Solaris 7.

Using csh and tcsh

By Paul DuBois
1st Edition August 1995
242 pages, ISBN 1-56592-132-1

Using csh and tcsh describes from
the beginning how to use these
shells interactively to get your work
done faster with less typing. You'll
learn how to make your prompt tell
you where you are (no more pwd);
use what you've typed before (history); type long command lines with
few keystrokes (command and file
name completion); remind yourself
of filenames when in the middle of
typing a command; and edit a botched
command without retyping it.

O'REILLY®

Learning GNU Emacs, 2nd Edition

By Debra Cameron, Bill Rosenblatt &
Eric Raymond
2nd Edition September 1996
560 pages, ISBN 1-56592-152-6

Learning GNU Emacs is an introduction to Version 19.30 of the GNU Emacs editor, one of the most widely used and powerful editors available under Unix. It provides a solid introduction to basic editing, a look at several important "editing modes" (special Emacs features for editing specific types of documents, including email, Usenet News, and the World Wide Web), and a brief introduction to customization and Emacs LISP programming. The book is aimed at new Emacs users, whether or not they are programmers. Includes quick-reference card.

Learning the vi Editor, 6th Edition

By Linda Lamb & Arnold Robbins
6th Edition October 1998
348 pages, ISBN 1-56592-426-6

This completely updated guide to editing with vi, the editor available on nearly every Unix system, now covers four popular vi clones and includes command summaries for easy reference. It starts with the basics, followed by more advanced editing tools, such as ex commands, global search and replacement, and a new feature, multi-screen editing.

Learning the bash Shell, 2nd Edition

By Cameron Newham &
Bill Rosenblatt
2nd Edition January 1998
336 pages, ISBN 1-56592-347-2

This second edition covers all of the features of bash Version 2.0, while still applying to bash Version 1.x. It includes one-dimensional arrays, parameter expansion, more pattern-matching operations, new commands, security improvements, additions to ReadLine, improved configuration and installation, and an additional programming aid, the bash shell debugger.

GNU Emacs Pocket Reference

By Debra Cameron
1st Edition November 1998
64 pages, ISBN 1-56592-496-7

O'Reilly's *Learning GNU Emacs* covers the most popular and widespread of the Emacs family of editors. The *GNU Emacs Pocket Reference* is a companion volume to *Learning GNU Emacs*. This small book, covering Emacs version 20, is a handy reference guide to the basic elements of this powerful editor, presenting the Emacs commands in an easy-to-use tabular format.

O'REILLY®

sed & awk, 2nd Edition

By Dale Dougherty & Arnold Robbins
2nd Edition March 1997
432 pages, ISBN 1-56592-225-5

sed & awk describes two text manipulation programs that are mainstays of the Unix programmer's toolbox. This edition covers the sed and awk programs as they are mandated by the POSIX standard and includes discussion of the GNU versions of these programs.

Effective awk Programming, 3rd Edition

By Arnold Robbins
3rd Edition May 2001
448 pages, ISBN 0-596-00070-7

Effective awk Programming delivers complete coverage of the awk 3.1 language and the most up-to-date coverage of the POSIX standard for awk available anywhere. Author Arnold Robbins clearly distinguishes standard awk features from GNU awk (gawk)–specific features, shines light into many of the "dark corners" of the language and devotes two full chapters to example programs. This book is the official "User's Guide" for the GNU implementation of awk.

sed & awk Pocket Reference, 2nd Edition

By Arnold Robbins
Second Edition June 2002
64 pages, 0-596-00352-8

The *sed & awk Pocket Reference* is a handy, quick reference guide to frequently used functions, commands, and regular expressions used for day-to-day text processing needs. This book is a companion to both *sed & awk*, Second Edition and *Effective awk Programming*, Third Edition.

Evil Geniuses in a Nutshell

By Illiad
1st Edition April 2000
132 pages, ISBN 1-56592-861-X

The follow-up to the highly successful first collection of *User Friendly* comic strips, *Evil Geniuses in a Nutshell* tells the continuing tale of Columbia Internet, "the friendliest, hardest-working and most neurotic little Internet Service Provider in the world." *User Friendly* reads like Dilbert for the Open Source community. It provides outsiders a light-hearted look at the world of the hard core geek and allows those who make their living dwelling in this world a chance to laugh at themselves.

The UNIX CD Bookshelf, Version 2.1

By O'Reilly & Associates, Inc.
Version 2.1 February 2000
624 pages, Features CD-ROM
ISBN 0-596-00000-6

The second edition of *The UNIX CD Bookshelf* contains six books from O'Reilly, plus the software from *UNIX Power Tools*—all on a convenient CD-ROM. Buyers also get a bonus hard-copy book, *UNIX in a Nutshell*, 3rd Edition. The CD-ROM contains *UNIX in a Nutshell*, 3rd Edition; *UNIX Power Tools*, 2nd Edition (with software); *Learning the UNIX Operating System*, 4th Edition; *Learning the vi Editor*, 6th Edition; *sed & awk*, 2nd Edition; and *Learning the Korn Shell*.

Managing Projects with make, 2nd Edition

By Andrew Oram & Steve Talbott
2nd Edition October 1991
152 pages, ISBN 0-937175-90-0

make is one of Unix's greatest contributions to software development, and this book is the clearest description of make ever written. It describes all the basic features and provides guidelines on meeting the needs of large, modern projects. Also contains a description of free products that contain major enhancements to make.

sed & awk, 2nd Edition

By Dale Dougherty & Arnold Robbins
2nd Edition March 1997
432 pages, ISBN 1-56592-225-5

sed & awk describes two text manipulation programs that are mainstays of the Unix programmer's toolbox. This edition covers the sed and awk programs as they are mandated by the POSIX standard and includes discussion of the GNU versions of these programs.

Writing GNU Emacs Extensions

By Bob Glickstein
1st Edition April 1997
236 pages, ISBN 1-56592-261-1

This book introduces Emacs Lisp and tells you how to make the editor do whatever you want, whether it's altering the way text scrolls or inventing a whole new "major mode." Topics progress from simple to complex, from lists, symbols, and keyboard commands to syntax tables, macro templates, and error recovery.

lex & yacc, 2nd Edition

By John Levine, Tony Mason &
Doug Brown
2nd Edition October 1992
366 pages, ISBN 1-56592-000-7

Shows programmers how to use two
Unix utilities, lex and yacc, in program development. You'll find tutori-
al sections for novice users, reference
sections for advanced users, and a
detailed index. Major MS-DOS and
Unix versions of lex and yacc are
explored in depth. Also covers Bison
and Flex.

Unix Power Tools, 3rd Edition

By Shelley Powers, Jerry Peek, Tim
O'Reilly & Mike Loukides
3rd Edition October 2002 (est.)
1512 pages (est.), ISBN 0-596-00330-7

In addition to vital information on
Linux, Darwin and BSD, *Unix Power
Tools*, 3rd Edition now offers more
coverage of bash, zsh and other new
shells, along with discussions on
modern utilities and applications.
Several sections focus on security
and Internet access, acknowledging
that most Unix boxes are connected
to the Internet. And there is a new
chapter on access to Unix from Windows, addressing the heterogeneous
nature of systems today.

O'REILLY®

To order: *800-998-9938* • *order@oreilly.com* • *www.oreilly.com*
Online editions of most O'Reilly titles are available by subscription at *safari.oreilly.com*
Also available at most retail and online bookstores.